CESAR CHAVEZ

LABOR LEADER

MARIA E. CEDEÑO

Consultants:

Dr. Julian Nava
Historian
Former U.S. Ambassador to Mexico

Yolanda Quintanilla-Finley
Teacher and Project Specialist
Corona Unified School District
Corona, California

Hispanic Heritage
The Millbrook Press
Brookfield, Connecticut

Cover photo courtesy of UPI/Bettmann
Photos courtesy of UPI/Bettmann: pp. 3, 4, 16, 25, 27, 28;
Archives of Labor and Urban Affairs, Wayne State University:
pp. 7, 13, 19; AP/Wide World Photos: pp. 10, 14, 20, 23, 26, 29.

Library of Congress Cataloging-in-Publication Data

Cedeño, Maria E., 1948–
Cesar Chavez : labor leader / by Maria E. Cedeño.
p.   cm.—(Hispanic heritage)
Includes bibliographical references and index.
Summary: Traces the accomplishments of the labor leader who fought
to improve the lives of Mexican-American farm workers in California.
ISBN 1-56294-280-8 (lib. bdg.)
1. Chavez, Cesar, 1927—Juvenile literature.   2. Labor leaders—
United States—Biography—Juvenile literature.   3. Trade-unions—
Migrant agricultural laborers—United States—Officials and
employees—Biography—Juvenile literature.   4. Mexican Americans—
Biography—Juvenile literature.   5. United Farm Workers—History—
Juvenile literature. [1. Chavez, Cesar, 1927–   .   2. Labor
leaders.   3. Migrant labor.   4. United Farm Workers—History.
5. Mexican Americans—Biography.]   I. Title.   II. Series.
HD6509.C48C43   1993
331.88'13'092—dc20
[B]   92-22620   CIP   AC

Published by The Millbrook Press
2 Old New Milford Road
Brookfield, Connecticut 06804

CESAR CHAVEZ

Union leader Cesar Chavez breaks bread with Robert Kennedy
at the end of his twenty-five-day fast.

On *February 14, 1968,* Cesar Chavez stopped eating. He did not put any food in his mouth for twenty-five days. Even though he was only forty-one years old, he got so weak that other people had to carry him. His weight dropped from 175 to 140 pounds (79 to 63 kilograms).

Chavez fasted—that is, he did without food—for a cause. He had been fighting to improve the lives of Mexican-American farm workers in California for many years. He was the leader of a union—an organization to support workers—called the United Farm Workers Organizing Committee. Its members were trying to give power to migrant workers, people who lived in run-down shacks and moved from town to town picking crops in farmers' fields. No matter how hard they worked, these people earned so little money that they could barely survive.

Chavez believed that the best way to call attention to these conditions was through nonviolent protest. His fast was a way to make the cry of the workers be heard by all Americans.

People worried because Chavez got very weak. But he kept on fasting because he wanted to prove his point. Senator Robert F. Kennedy came to visit him on the twenty-fifth day, when Chavez, at the advice of his doctors, finally agreed to break his fast. Kennedy said, "The world must know that the migrant farm worker, the Mexican American, is coming into his own right."

Chavez's act was very dramatic. The whole nation looked on. Many people supported him. They were filled with sympathy for this brave man and the cause of the farm workers.

But the struggle was not over. The people who owned the farms were very determined. So was Cesar Chavez, and it was he and the people who joined him who would little by little win the rights that the workers deserved.

IN THE GILA VALLEY · Cesar Estrada Chavez was born on March 31, 1927, in a room above a store in the Gila Valley near Yuma, Arizona. His father, Librado Chavez, owned a business—which included the store with living quarters above it—and worked on his own parents' ranch.

Cesar's grandfather and namesake, Cesar, was the head of the large Chavez family. His family called him Papa Chayo. Sometime during the 1880s, he had escaped from a huge ranch in northern Mexico where he had been a slave. He crossed the Rio Grande river to

Texas, where he worked very hard to save enough money so that his wife, Tella, and their fourteen children could join him.

The couple moved to the North Gila Valley near the Colorado River, where they homesteaded more than one hundred acres along the valley floor. This meant that by living and working on the land, they made it their own.

The Chavez family home in the Gila Valley, Arizona, was deserted in 1960.

One by one the children grew up, got married, and started their own families. By 1924, Librado was the only Chavez child at home. At the age of thirty-eight he married Cesar's mother, Juana Estrada, a small-boned Mexican woman with strong beliefs. A year later, their first baby was born, a girl whom they named Rita. Two years later, little Cesar was born. In time, Rita and Cesar would have four more brothers and sisters. Ricardo, who was called Richard, was closest in age to Cesar. The two boys would stay best friends for life.

When Cesar turned seven, he went to the valley school. He had a hard time picking up English words, which were foreign to the Chavez family, who only spoke Spanish at home. He hated combing his hair in the morning and getting dressed in clean clothes and stiff, unfamiliar shoes. He found it hard to sit still all day behind his old wooden desk until he heard his favorite sound—the dismissal bell.

The Chavez children received an informal education, too, from their uncles, grandmother, and especially their mother. Uncle Ramon would sit Cesar on his lap, give him a piece of candy or a soda, and read to him in Spanish. Cesar loved the sounds of the words. He would like Spanish more than English all his life.

Cesar's mother was a strong believer in the Catholic faith. She taught her children to pray every morning and night and to love and obey God. She told them stories, and she often used Spanish *dichos,* or sayings, to teach them how they should live. She would say, "If you do not learn from advice, you will not reach old age." She taught her sons not to fight. Her favorite *dicho* was, "You need two to fight, and one can't do it alone."

Juana was against violence, but what she disliked even more was selfishness. She taught her children to think of others. At dinnertime, if one of the children complained about getting the smallest serving, Juana would take the food from the table. The children learned to say, "Well, I got the smallest portion, but it doesn't matter."

Cesar never forgot his mother's lessons. More than anything, he remembered that love was to share with others.

MOVING ON · All through his childhood, Cesar heard his parents talk about the difficult times that the United States was going through. Families were poor, and they did not have money to buy the food and clothing they needed. In the 1930s, America sank into the Great Depression, a time of great hardship for people all over America.

Cesar's father lost his business, and he had to move his family back to the Chavez farm. Then a bad drought turned the fertile soil back into desert. One day in 1937, when Cesar was ten years old, his parents said that they had to give up the farm in the valley.

In August 1938, Librado and Juana Chavez and their children packed their belongings and left the home that Papa Chayo had built many years before. With only forty dollars in his pocket, Librado Chavez drove his family to California, where he had heard that there was work.

In southern California, the Chavez family met with labor contractors, men who looked for migrant, or seasonal, workers for large farms. The workers would go to a farm to pick fruits and vegetables during the harvest.

Migrant worker shacks in the San Joaquin valley, southern California.

Then they would move on to another farm whose crops were ripe and ready to pick. The contractors told the Chavez family that they could earn a lot of money picking crops.

At last the family found work on a large farm. They were directed to a tiny old shack made of aluminum sheets. It was hard to believe, but this was where they were supposed to live. There was only one dirty room, no bathroom, and a hot plate for cooking. The family took mattresses and pots and pans out of their old Studebaker. Cesar found some water and gave it to his mother so that she could prepare the evening meal.

Cesar never forgot that night. He began to collect all the information he could about the unfair treatment of migrant workers. Many of them were Mexicans or Mexican Americans like him. Without an education or special training in any field and often with very little knowledge of English, they had few choices in life. His heart reached out to his people. One day, perhaps, he would be able to help.

MIGRANT LIFE · The Chavez family stayed on that farm until the cotton harvest was over. When they got their pay, they were shocked. The contractor paid them much less money than he had promised them. Their English wasn't good enough to protest, and in the end, they took the money and drove on.

They headed for northern California, where they had heard that the pay was higher. They picked beans for fifty cents a basket. They chased the crops from Sacramento and San Jose in the north to the Imperial Valley in the south. Everyone picked—grapes, prunes, cucumbers, and tomatoes in summer, and cotton from October to Christmas.

At times, they could not afford to rent a room. Then the family had to crowd into the Studebaker to sleep. Since there were so many of them, Cesar and Richard would sleep on an old mattress on the ground.

During the winter, Juana and Librado Chavez tried to stay in one place so that their children could go to school. This was almost impossible, though, because the crops were already picked, and the money they had saved from the harvest was not enough to see them through.

School for Cesar was a nightmare. By the time he had reached eighth grade, he had gone to more than thirty-seven of them. On the first day of school in Fresno, he was deeply hurt. The principal of the school kept Cesar and Richard in the office all morning without placing them in a class. He said terrible things about Mexican-American children. None of the teachers wanted them in their classroom, he said. Cesar was hurt and confused. How could this man dislike them so much when he didn't even know them?

Cesar Chavez graduated from the eighth grade in 1942.

FROM ANGER TO ACTION · Years went by, and Cesar became a responsible young man. The Chavez family was finally able to stay put in one place. They rented an old cottage near San Jose, California. Since there were a lot of large farms in that area, they hoped the work would be steady. Cesar began to work in the vineyards. He loved to watch the vines and grapes grow, but the work was very hard. He had to bend over for hours at a time, and this made his back hurt. Gnats would stick on his face and arms in hot weather.

Migrant workers stoop over fields in the hot sun for hours on end.

He began to talk to the other workers about asking the growers for better housing and wages. Most workers had families to feed, so they were afraid to anger their bosses by asking for anything. Many of them would not listen to Cesar. But he kept talking.

When Cesar was fifteen years old, he met Helen Fabela. She was a pretty girl close to his own age who wore flowers in her hair. Cesar would go to the grocery store where Helen worked every chance he could get. Then they started to date.

During this time, the United States was fighting World War II. Cesar, who turned seventeen in 1944, decided to join the navy. He hated the time he spent in the service. People discriminated against him, or treated him badly because of his ethnic background.

When Cesar returned home after two years of duty, the discrimination did not end. One time, he and Helen went to the movies and sat in seats reserved for whites. The ushers asked them to move. Cesar refused. The police arrested him, but since he had not broken a law, they had to let him go. Cesar became even more certain that he had to do something about the discrimination suffered by Mexican Americans.

In 1948, Helen and Cesar were married. After a honeymoon spent touring California's Spanish missions in his father's Studebaker, Cesar and his bride returned to their own house in Delano—a one-room shack without electricity or running water. The only heat came from a kerosene stove. Since they had no car, Cesar would hitchhike to and from the fields each day.

In that same year, Cesar Chavez became involved in his first strike. The migrant laborers walked out of the fields in protest of the unfair working conditions and low pay. After only a few days, though, the workers went back to the fields. Nothing had changed.

Three of the one hundred starving children found in a migrant camp in 1950.

But Chavez believed even more that change was possible. He began to read about people who had spent their lives helping others. He especially admired the great Indian leader Mahatma Gandhi, who had used nonviolent protest to overthrow British rule in India.

Chavez kept trying to persuade the other workers to join together and demand a pay raise. But people were still too afraid of losing their jobs. Then he began teaching Mexican migrant workers how to speak English. If they knew English, they could take the steps to become American citizens. If they were citizens, they would not have to fear being deported, or sent back to Mexico.

People began to hear about the work Chavez was doing. Fred Ross was among them. He came to visit Chavez in June 1952. But Chavez did not want to meet this man. He was sure that Ross was just another *gringo*— a slang name that Mexicans use for white people. Helen insisted, though, that Ross only wanted to help the workers. Finally, Chavez agreed to meet him. Years later, Chavez would say of Ross, "He changed my life."

JOINING TOGETHER · Ross told Chavez about the group he had formed called the Community Service Organization (CSO). This group wanted to help migrant farm workers by making their communities better places in which to live. Chavez was very moved. He later said, "He [Fred Ross] did such a good job of explaining how poor people could build power that I could even taste it, I could *feel* it."

The following evening, Chavez started working for the CSO. He helped Ross register migrants to vote. After a long day in the lumberyard, where he was working at the time, Chavez walked for hours, knocking on door after door, telling people that they must vote. If Mexican Americans began to vote, they would have an influence on politics. People would listen to them, he said. Ross was impressed with the young man's intelligence and energy. "I think I've found the guy I'm looking for," he wrote.

Chavez held meetings in different workers' homes. He helped people by interpreting for them when they didn't speak English; he wrote letters for them when they couldn't write; he told them how to deal with difficult situations. People in the San Jose area heard about Cesar Chavez. His name began to command respect.

Ross hired Chavez to work for the CSO in Oakland, California. Chavez made his first speeches in front of large groups. He traveled all over California—to Madera, Bakersfield, Hanford, and Oxnard. "Everywhere there were problems," Chavez said. "But no matter what happened, I learned."

Then in 1959, Chavez left the CSO and returned to Delano. He and Helen had saved $1,200. With this money they formed a new organization called the National Farm

Helen Chavez helped her husband in his effort to improve the lives of farm workers through a strong union.

Workers Association (NFWA). Their goal was to help organize the migrant workers of the San Joaquin Valley. Chavez spent several years driving around to the fields, talking to the workers and gaining their confidence. He never questioned the importance of his belief. "You must stay with one thing," he said, "and just hammer away, hammer away, and it will happen."

DOLORES HUERTA
AND *LA CAUSA*

In 1962 Cesar Chavez talked Dolores Huerta into joining the National Farm Workers Association. She would become a leading union spokesperson and organizer.

At the time, she had six children and was about to give birth to a seventh. It was hard for her to be both a mother and an active member of a union. But as a Chicana (the name given to Mexican and Mexican-American women) and a migrant worker, Huerta had felt the sting of discrimination. She believed strongly in the cause—*la causa.*

Chavez wanted women to work in the union. He asked them to be leaders. Huerta said, "Women have gotten stronger because he [Chavez] expects so much of us." One reason that Chavez wanted women to join men on the picket lines was that he wanted the protest to remain nonviolent. If women and children were there, people would be less likely to hurt each other.

Dolores Huerta (center) leads a rally with Howard Wallace and Maria Elena Chavez, daughter of Cesar Chavez.

By 1962, when he had talked three hundred people into joining, he called a meeting. His cousin Manuel designed a red flag with a black Aztec eagle inside a white circle. Chavez said of the flag, "To me it looks like a strong, beautiful sign of hope."

More and more workers joined the NFWA. It seemed as though Chavez's dream about the day when migrant farm workers had the same rights as all American workers was on its way to coming true.

HUELGA! · By 1965 the grape pickers on a large ranch in Delano had had enough. They earned about a dollar an hour. There were no toilets in the fields for them, and the few that were on the ranch were very dirty. The pickers worked in extreme heat with no protection, fighting the bugs and breathing in the dangerous chemicals called pesticides that the farmers used to protect their crops.

On September 7 the workers went on strike. They refused to keep picking grapes without a raise in pay. Cesar did not want to join the strike because he did not think that the NFWA was well enough organized to be a success.

But the pickers insisted. On September 16, Mexican Independence Day, in spite of Chavez's fears, the NFWA voted to help the workers.

Once he had decided to join, Chavez did all that he could. More than a thousand workers formed picket lines around the grape fields of Delano, holding signs with pictures of the NFWA eagle on them. As they marched along, they invited people working in the fields to join them, and they cried, *"Huelga! Huelga!"*—the Spanish word for strike.

The growers did not budge, and the strike went on. Then Chavez had an idea. He began a campaign to ask the American people not to buy grapes. He asked supermarket owners, businesspeople, and American workers to support the migrant workers in their struggle for better wages. People listened. The boycott, or organized refusal, spread throughout the country and even the world. Other powerful unions and groups added their voice to the protest.

In 1966 the United States Senate Subcommittee on Migratory Labor came to Delano to look into the situation. Robert Kennedy gave his total support to the union cause. He and Chavez became friends.

Next, sixty-seven union members decided to go on a 250-mile-long (400-kilometer) march from Delano all the way to the state capital in Sacramento. On Easter Sunday, with aching legs and blisters on their feet, they arrived. Ten thousand people had gathered to greet them.

Striking NFWA grape pickers walk through a vineyard on their way to Sacramento in March 1966.

On the capitol steps, Chavez announced that the grape growers had agreed to the workers' demands. The union had won a contract with Schenley Industries, the company that owned the Delano vineyards. This contract was the first of its kind in the history of American farm labor.

THE POWER OF NONVIOLENCE · The battle for fair treatment was not over. Schenley was only one of the large companies that owned the farms around Delano. Then another barrier was put in front of the strikers. The Teamsters, led by Jimmy Hoffa, was a very powerful union representing truckers and other industries. Threatened by the growing strength of the migrants, Hoffa began to compete with the NFWA for its members.

Cesar Chavez had another great idea. He built a little chapel inside his station wagon where he held vigils day and night. Workers came in from the fields and talked to union members. More and more people joined the NFWA side.

Then Chavez decided that the NFWA needed more support. The NFWA joined with the Agricultural Workers Organizing Committee. This large union was backed by the oldest and strongest group of unions in the country, the AFL–CIO. The new organization was called the United Farm Workers Organizing Committee (UFWOC).

In February 1968, Cesar Chavez began to fast. This would be the first of three times when he would stop eating in protest of the working conditions and low pay of the farm workers. His dramatic act did not immediately solve the problems of the workers, but the entire country was moved by his bravery and the reason for his fast.

Cesar Chavez, weakened by his fast, is helped to a Mass in his honor.

In 1973 a strike was called for higher wages from lettuce growers. This time things got very rough. The Teamsters attacked the strikers. The United Farm Workers of America (UFW), as the UFWOC was now called, used up $3 million from the AFL–CIO strike fund, and still the lettuce growers refused to talk.

Finally, in 1974, the new governor of California, Jerry Brown, put through the Agricultural Labor Relations Act, a bill of rights for farm workers—the first ever in the United States. From then on, farm workers had the right to organize. In August 1975, people voted on whether they wanted the Teamsters or the UFW to represent farm workers. The UFW won by a long shot.

When Chavez merged the NFWA with the AFL-CIO to form the United Farm Workers, the result was a much more powerful union.

"UNTIL THE FIELDS ARE SAFE" · Cesar Chavez did not stop helping migrant workers. During the 1980s, the UFWCO became very concerned with the dangers of pesticides in grape orchards for the people who worked there. The workers went on strike.

In 1986 Chavez led a new boycott in protest of the use of toxic pesticides on grapes.

*Left to right:
Ethel Kennedy,
Helen Chavez,
Cesar Chavez, Juana
Chavez (Cesar's
mother), and Jesse
Jackson on the last
day of Chavez's
1988 fast.*

Chavez fasted a third time in 1988, at sixty-one years old, in protest of the use of these poisons. He fasted for thirty-six days. This was very bad for his health. Twenty years had passed since the first time he stopped eating to show the world how much the farm workers suffered and needed their help. Ethel Kennedy, Robert Kennedy's widow, was there with several of their children. Juana, Cesar Chavez's ninety-six-year-old mother, sat by his side.

Chavez's son Fernando read a statement written by his father. The last words were, "And the fast will endure until the fields are safe for farm workers, the environment is preserved for future generations, and our food is once again a source of nourishment and life."

Cesar Chavez promised to continue the fight.

Cesar Chavez has won many battles, but the war against poverty and squalid working conditions is far from over.

IMPORTANT EVENTS IN
THE LIFE OF CESAR CHAVEZ

1927   Cesar Chavez is born on March 31 near Yuma, Arizona.

1938   Cesar's family loses its farm and moves to California to seek work as migrant farm workers.

1944   Cesar joins the U.S. Navy during World War II.

1948   Cesar Chavez and Helen Fabela marry and move to Delano, California. Cesar becomes involved in his first farm workers' strike.

1952   Chavez starts working for the Community Service Organization.

1959   Cesar and Helen Chavez form the National Farm Workers Association.

1965   Chavez leads a strike of grape pickers in California.

1966   Chavez leads a 250-mile march of union members to Sacramento, California's state capital. He announces that the grape pickers have won the strike. In August, his union becomes part of the AFL-CIO and is called the United Farm Workers Organizing Committee.

1968   Chavez fasts to protest the poor working conditions and low pay of farm workers.

1974   California passes a law giving farm workers many rights, including the right to organize.

1988   Cesar Chavez fasts to protest the use of dangerous pesticides in the fields.

FIND OUT MORE
ABOUT CESAR CHAVEZ

Cesar Chavez by Ruth Franchere. New York: HarperCollins Children's Books, 1986.

Cesar Chavez by Consuelo Rodriguez. New York: Chelsea House, 1991.

Cesar Chavez and La Causa by Maurice Roberts. Chicago, Ill.: Childrens Press, 1986.

INDEX